A special thank-you for

_____

You have made a difference in my life.
Thank you for your encouragement.

With gratitude,

_____

Date

_____

Our purpose at Howard Publishing is to:
- *Increase faith* in the hearts of growing Christians
- *Inspire holiness* in the lives of believers
- *Instill hope* in the hearts of struggling people everywhere

Because He's coming again!

Published by Howard Publishing Co., Inc.
3117 North 7th Street, West Monroe, Louisiana 71291-2227

03 04 05 06 07 08 09 10 11 12   10 9 8 7 6 5 4 3 2 1

Stories by Caron Chandler Loveless
Edited by Between the Lines
Interior design by LinDee Loveland and Stephanie Denney

ISBN: 1-58229-310-4

thank you

for your

encouragement

a collection of poems,
prayers, stories, quotes, and
scriptures to say thank you

HOWARD
PUBLISHING CO.

thank you

As a lighthouse

to ships at

sea, your

encouragement

has been

a beacon to

guide me.

thank **you**

for your
encouragement

for your encouragement

Dear _____,

Above all the noise that clutters my life, it's your words I hear. When I doubt, you park yourself firmly in my corner— cheering, believing, and helping me bounce back from the ropes of my insecurity. You've listened to my complaints, eased my fears, and supported my plans. Your encouraging words have been like fuel for my soul. They give me the fire I need to stay the course and finish the race well.

Never think your acts have gone unobserved or are unworthy of mention. Your kind support has been noticed— and not only by me but by God, who knows all, sees all, and flings wide the window of blessing for you because of the blessing you've been to me and others.

Thanks to your encouraging influence, I am stronger, richer, and surer today. You've helped me feel like a winner—but the prize truly belongs to you. Thank you for encouraging me!

With deep appreciation,

Philemon
7

NIV

YOUR LOVE
HAS GIVEN
ME GREAT
JOY AND
ENCOURAGEMENT.

Through grief and through danger
Thy smile hath cheer'd my way,
Till hope seem'd to bud
From each thorn that round me lay.

— *Thomas Moore*

Labor Day Shoes

Mindee was nearly in tears as she strolled through the mall. Ankles swollen and throbbing, she was just weeks away from the event she had anticipated for years. After years of futile attempts to become pregnant, finally her baby—the child doctors said she might never hold—was almost within her grasp. But now that Mindee was on her own—and about to become a single mom—she felt more stressed than ever. How would she provide for this child? How could she ever afford to give him all those sweet little things every mother wants her baby to have?

Maybe the mall isn't such a good idea today, Mindee thought with a sigh. Browsing in baby departments and longing for fleecy crib sets, ultrasafe car seats, and adorable newborn clothes were putting her in a bad mood. The more she walked, the more envy she felt toward every woman pushing a stroller full of shopping bags. Trying to finish college, Mindee had only thirty dollars to her name. To her, the prospects for financial improvement seemed about a galaxy away.

This wasn't at all the life Mindee had envisioned. She had tried to be a good wife. She did her best to be positive, even when her husband escalated the arguments that had increasingly flared up between them. She took great care to do everything the way her husband wanted, hoping to avoid conflict. As their relationship fell into a death spiral, Mindee suggested marriage counseling. But her husband refused. He just wanted out.

In the flurry of grief and confusion that followed, Mindee decided that if she was ever going to make it on her own, she would need to do two things: one was to go back to school; the other was to go back to church.

That's where Mindee met Ruth. Ruth was one of those chirpy, bright-eyed women who seemed never to meet a stranger. She was an exceptionally good listener and a prize-winning gardener, not to mention she was generally regarded as the best alto in the church choir. From the first night the two women shared a music book, things just clicked. Each knew she had found a soul mate.

For Mindee, Ruth was a godsend. When the newcomer felt shy, Ruth drew her into the social scene. The day Mindee's husband filed for divorce, Ruth showed up with a tender heart and plenty of tissues. And Ruth had been there two months later, when Mindee phoned, hysterical: "Ruth, you are not going to believe this. I'm pregnant! The doctor just confirmed it. Can you believe this is finally happening, *now?!* The timing is terrible!" Ruth had taken in the bitter-sweet news, calming Mindee and rejoicing with her over the new little life, talking her through morning sickness, and offering to share her own maternity clothes.

Even though Ruth's friendship had been a lifeline, today Mindee felt miserable. As she moped her way out of the mall, she passed an exclusive children's clothing store; glancing through the window, she spied a tiny pair of athletic shoes perched on display. They were precious little shoes. No. They were perfect. The exact kind of shoes Mindee had always hoped her baby might wear. What would it hurt to step inside for a closer look?

Mindee cradled the shoes in her palm, her eyes lighting up as she wondered at the tiny feet that would fit them. Her taut, puffy fingers traced the canvas of bright, primary colors as she tried to picture what her little one might look like wearing them.

"Is there something I can help you with, ma'am?" asked the clerk, looking up from the counter.

"Oh, no," Mindee answered, trying to sound disinterested. "I was just admiring these cute little athletic shoes in the window."

"You have good taste," the man said with approval. "Those are our top sellers."

"I can see why they would be," Mindee answered, then waited for the clerk to redirect his attention elsewhere.

Discreetly searching for a price tag, Mindee flipped the shoes over. Her heart nearly fell through the floor. Like everything else these days, the shoes were priced way out of her reach. She couldn't spend that much for her own shoes, much less a baby's. Mindee plopped the shoes back on the display and headed for the door.

Labor Day Shoes

"Is there something else we can show you?" the clerk asked before she could slip away.

"Not today, I guess," she answered, avoiding the man's gaze.

"Maybe next time then."

"Yeah, maybe next time." Mindee tried to suppress the rising desperation, the notion that she'd never be able to afford nice things for her baby.

Snap out of this, will you? Mindee scolded herself as she walked to her car. *Why can't you just be thankful for what you do have? It's not the end of the world that you can't afford an expensive pair of shoes. For goodness' sake, be happy.*

But the self-talk fell flat, and when she got home, Mindee devoured an entire freshly opened bag of Oreo cookies in a vain attempt at consolation. She was feeling more than a little depressed.

A few nights later, Ruth invited Mindee to her house to pick up a box of baby clothes. When Mindee arrived and the door swung open, she took a step back, stunned at the riotous shouts coming from the enthusiastic women inside: "Surprise!" "Happy Baby Shower!"

Mindee was pulled into the welcoming crowd and inundated with hugs and laughter. She felt a lump of emotion in her throat as she was ushered into a room filled wall-to-wall with choir women. Then she spotted Ruth standing next to what looked like an avalanche of gifts, beaming.

"I don't know what to say," Mindee cried, wiping mascara streaks from her face. She reached for Ruth's hand. "This whole thing must be your idea, huh?"

"It was me," Ruth answered, "and a couple of dozen other people who weren't about to just stand around doing nothing when there's a naked little boy about to be born!" Ruth laughed, then directed Mindee to the center of the room. A blue rocking chair stood waiting, decorated with a festive balloon bouquet. Nearby, a table swathed in blue lace was loaded with a triple-layer chocolate cake with baby blue frosting and a stack of gifts that overflowed onto the fireplace hearth.

The women howled and hooted as they played shower games. A boisterous quartet dressed in nurses' costumes performed for Mindee the never-before-heard song "Lullaby for Your Labor Day." Soon she was ankle-deep in giftwrapping.

Labor Day Shoes

Mindee paused to sip her lemonade and survey the sights and sounds in the cozy house. She basked in the warmth, thoughtfulness, and abundance flowing her way; and for the first time...maybe ever...Mindee knew she was feeling God's love.

Finally the last gift was handed to Mindee. It was neatly wrapped in crisp, yellow tissue paper and topped with a bow of baby blue ribbon with frisky lambs on it. Like a child relishing her dessert, Mindee slowed to savor this final gift. No card was attached to this one, so she asked around for the giver. Then she caught Ruth's sheepish grin. Mindee held her breath as she lifted the box lid and peeked inside, then suddenly let out a loud gasp.

"Oh, honey," Ruth teased. "Don't do that! You just might burst something!" Everyone laughed. Then the room grew still.

"Oh, Ruth!" Mindee exclaimed, still holding the box lid and feeling tears well up again. Nestled snugly in the box were the same tiny athletic shoes Mindee had wished for in the store window. "You have no idea! This is *exactly* what I wanted! I saw these just the other day, but there was no way on earth I could buy them and no way you could have known!"

Ruth's eyes shone too as she bent down to hug her friend. "I'm so relieved that you like them. When I went shopping, I fully intended to buy something else. But when I saw those cute little things, they just seemed to say, 'Pick me! Pick me!'"

Everyone agreed that they were special little shoes for the special little boy who was on his way.

When the party was over, Mindee felt exhausted but wonderfully refreshed. Later that night, in her cramped apartment, Mindee unpacked the flannel sheets, the ultrasafe car seat, and the darling newborn baby clothes. She pulled out her most treasured gift and looked for a spot to display the bright little shoes. It would be months before they would fit her child, but until that day they would serve a higher purpose: Each time she walked into the baby's room, they would be a sweet reminder that God knew her needs—and even her heart's desires. This gift was a promise, an encouragement that somehow, in His own way, God would help her take care of her baby.

Labor Day Shoes

thank
you

Your

encouragement

was God's gift

at just the

right time.

a blessing
for you

May ay you always feel supported,

*U*pheld in every way;

*F*or all the times you fanned my hopes,

*M*ay your heart be blessed today.

for your
encouragement

for your encouragement

May God be gracious to you,

His love to you impart;

May peace reign in your spirit

And joy overflow your heart.

thank
you

You lifted my

head and gave a

song of courage

and triumph to

my heart.

If I can stop one heart from breaking,
I shall not live in vain;
If I can ease one life the aching,
Or cool one pain,
Or help one fainting robin
Unto his nest again,
I shall not live in vain.

—*Emily Dickinson*

1 Thessalonians
5:11

NIV

ENCOURAGE
ONE ANOTHER
AND BUILD
EACH OTHER UP,
JUST AS
IN FACT
YOU ARE DOING.

Running into Friendship

Kaye was not exactly what you'd call an athlete. When she'd read about the race in the paper, the prospect of her participating seemed about as likely as a trip to the moon. But there she stood—fussing with a safety pin, trying to tack on her race number. All around her, seasoned athletes jumped, stretched, and rolled their necks. Kaye felt somewhat like an impostor.

"Hey there, Kaye." A voice broke into her thoughts. It was Denise. "You ready for this?"

"Hi!" Kaye responded, bending to check her shoelaces. "I'm as ready as I'm going to be, I guess."

"What kind of talk is that?" Denise scolded. "The 10Ks are a blast. Just think about all the calories you'll burn."

Running

"Right...fun," Kaye said, rolling her eyes and laughing.

"You're welcome to run with Missy, Tara, and me," Denise offered.

"Thanks. But I'd only slow you guys down."

"Well, look for me when it's over. I want to see how you did!" Denise called out as she headed toward the starting line.

"OK. Good luck."

Kaye had met Denise at the Track Hut, where Denise taught a runner's orientation class. In spite of a car accident ten years earlier that had left her a paraplegic, Denise was a true athlete. She had been a champion cross-country racer in college, and even though she now raced in a wheelchair, she and her friends shared a goal to enter the Boston Marathon. If Denise raced well today, she'd be on her way to meeting the six-hour qualifying time required to enter the Marathon.

Kaye, on the other hand, had taken up running to lose weight. She was so depressed about her appearance that she could hardly walk by a mirror without ruining her day. But she was starting to see progress, and it encouraged her to lace up her shoes each morning and keep at it. Preparing for this race had kept her focused and disciplined.

into Friendship

"All runners to the starting line," a voice announced over the loudspeaker. "The race will begin in three minutes."

Well, here goes, Kaye thought, clipping on her CD player and adjusting her headphones. She scanned the crowds and located her husband, Dan, and their two young children, waving banners and screaming their support.

"Runners, take your places," came the final warning. Kaye gave her family a wave, then joined the other runners.

A cheer went up from the spectators. It gave Kaye butterflies. She straightened up and listened for the gun.

Crack!

She was off. For the first mile, running seemed effortless. Adrenaline pulsed through her body, and she couldn't suppress her grin.

Kaye always used a CD player when she ran. The high-energy music motivated her. She couldn't run without it. She'd learned that running was largely a mind game, and music relieved the monotony, distracting her from the fatigue.

Just past mile two, something went wrong. *What in the world?* Kaye wondered. *Surely this isn't...I can't lose my music! I'll*

Running

never make it. But the volume on her CD player was fading fast. In all her excitement, she'd forgotten to check the batteries!

Kaye started to panic. If running 6.2 miles was hard *with* music, it would be impossible without it. Suddenly Kaye's legs felt like tree trunks. Her breath was short. She tried talking to herself: She had run this distance in practice—twice—and she could do it again. But her pep talk fell on deaf ears.

By the third mile, runners and cheering fans were sparse. Sweat stung Kaye's eyes. The warm air felt suffocating. Her music was gone, and so was Kaye's will to finish. She was just about to quit when she spotted Denise, downing an energy drink.

"Kaye...how's it going?" Denise asked.

"Not...good," Kaye panted. "My...CD...player...died."

"That's tough..." Denise sympathized between breaths. "Know the feeling. I've had some trouble too." Denise pointed down at her wheelchair. "Flat tire."

"Will...it affect your time?" Kaye asked, truly concerned.

"Sure," Denise said, trying to sound matter-of-fact. "But there are other races." Her face brightened. "Since my race is shot, why don't I hang back with you? Help get you in."

into Friendship

"No...really...I'll be fine," Kaye protested.

"You won't be fine. Look at you. This is your first race...and if I have anything to say, it won't be your last." Denise smiled encouragingly at Kaye. "Come on now, let's pick up that pace."

Denise was exactly the spark Kaye needed. She settled into an easy, rolling groove beside the gasping, grunting Kaye. Denise's taut, muscular arms shone with sweat as they grabbed and released, grabbed and released the silver rims of her wheelchair. What a marvel she was. Denise was paralyzed, but that hadn't squelched her dreams or slowed her drive.

In just minutes Kaye was striding easily as Denise coached her breathing and pace and offered encouragement. Soon they heard the thrilling sound of crowds at the finish line, and Denise saw Dan and the kids cheering.

Fueled by the sight of her family and Denise's support, Kaye felt a fresh surge of energy push her to sprint the last fifty yards.

"Go!" Denise shouted, as Kaye pulled ahead. "You've got it!"

Kaye could hear Denise cheering for her as she proudly crossed the finish line. Panting and wheezing, Kaye walked sev-

Running

eral blocks to cool down. As she turned to look for her family, Denise rolled up beside her.

"Where do you think you're going, young lady?" she asked in mock disapproval, then smiled.

"I need a camera," Kaye explained. "Dan's got the camera."

"For what?"

"I want a picture...with my hero here," Kaye said, indicating Denise. "I can't believe I did it!"

"*We* did it," Denise corrected softly. "And *we* can do it again. There's another race in three weeks, and since you made me lose my time today," she added, smiling, "you're just going to have to be there."

"*I* made you..." Kaye said, the truth just starting to sink in.

"It was just a minor problem with my chair," Denise admitted. "I still could have made a qualifying time. But how would it have looked if I had let you wimp out on us, rookie?"

Kaye grinned. "I owe you...big time. Thanks."

Denise and three friends did make it to the Boston Marathon. Two of her friends raced beside her in wheelchairs. But the third was happy just to cheer her on and jog the sidelines with her video camera.

into Friendship

thank
you

In the race of

life, your faithful

cheers help me

go the distance.

Encouragement
is oxygen
to the
soul.

GEORGE M. ADAMS

I do not wish you joy without sorrow,
Nor endless day without the healing
  dark,
Nor brilliant sun without the restful
  shadow,
Nor tides that never turn against your
  bark.
I wish you love, and strength, and faith,
  and wisdom,
Goods, gold enough to help some needy
  one.
I wish you songs, but also blessed silence,
And God's sweet peace when every day
  is done.

—*Dorothy Nell McDonald*

thank you

Without your

encouragement,

I might have

given up. Thank

you for coming

alongside and

helping me to

keep going.

thank
you

for your
encouragement

Dear Heavenly Father,

Shower Your favor on this dear one who has so faithfully encouraged me. Sustain her selfless spirit by Your almighty power and refresh her now to the depths of her soul. Refresh her with streams of encouragement that ripple with whispers from Your heart. Surprise her with sweet moments from You.

Please grant her the most secret desires of her heart—the ones only You and she know about. Fill her with joy at knowing that someone else has prospered and been helped through the sound of her voice and the touch of her hand. Be near to her, Lord, and grant her true peace. Illuminate her mind with Your Word. Reveal to her the hidden treasures You've reserved just for her. And by the power of Your great love, keep her safe in the palm of Your ever-steady hand.

Amen.

You never know
when a moment
and a few sincere
words can have an
impact on a life.

ZIG ZIGLAR